CREDIT REPAIR SECRETS

*The 10 Ways To Fix Your Credit & Completely Turn
Bad Credit Into Good Credit*

MICHAEL GREENE

CONTENTS

Introduction

Banks and other lending institutions always check your background before giving you loans or credit. A low credit score is a common reason for credit denial.

This e-book is a comprehensive guide towards understanding how credit scores work and how to fix them fast.

We will first discuss what credit ratings are and their importance to your financial life. Chapter 2 explains the components in calculating your credit score and clarifies common misconceptions about it. One special part of chapter 2 will explain why credit repair companies are a scam.

Next, we will tackle factors that contribute to low credit scores. Finally, the last chapter is a guide towards saving your credit score from plummeting and then rebuilding it back to restore your stability.

It's recommended to read the first three chapters to fully comprehend the steps we'll take in fixing your credit rating.

What Is Credit?

❧❦❧

I n today's time, living without credit is hard. We use credit to get houses, cars and smart phones. Quite surprisingly, people blindly swipe their credit cards, without having any second thoughts.

Sadly, people only realize the size of their debt when they're left with no choice but to foreclose their homes. Others have problems getting employed due to their credit history.

Your transactions are recorded and compiled in a credit report, which banks refer to in deciding whether to approve your loan application. Building good financial behavior is a crucial step towards applying for a loan. Also, being aware of your financial behavior leads to better debt.

There are different modes of payment for goods. The two most common are cash and credit. Cash is a full payment in exchange for a product while credit is a deferred payment between you, the seller and the bank. The bank pays the seller for your purchase while you repay the bank in the future. Usually, the amount repaid has interest depending on the length of your payment.

Payments for credit also vary, from paying the debt off in full to periodic small payments that gradually decrease your outstanding balance.

However, small items, like appliances and gadgets, are not the only ones that can be paid through credit. Your house, car and even business also involve getting long-term loans. These kinds of credit are the most useful, but also the most dangerous because of the amount involved.

Credit Scores

If you get several loans at the same time while using a credit card, then your debt balloons so high that you will end up having no capacity to pay. Even if a few obligations are discharged, you find it impossible to pay them all.

Let's assume that you did manage to get rid of all your debt somehow. You finally get the courage to apply for a credit card. Sadly, the bank rejected your application, so you applied for another. Still, you got rejected and you finally noticed the problem—your credit score.

Before a bank gives you a credit card, they think about your financial behavior. Banks run a risk assessment to be sure that you'll pay back what you borrowed. Being responsible with credit is a deciding factor for you to get an approved application.

For quick reference, banks use credit scores to assess you. A credit score is a three-figure grade given to consumers that measures their creditworthiness or ability to pay back the amount borrowed.

Your credit score, since it is a quantitative basis of your

debt, needs to be based on real information about your financial history. A credit report is the primary resource of credit scores, which we will tackle in detail later.

The FICO score from the Fair Isaac Corporation is the usual credit score that most lenders use. The FICO score ranges from 300 to 850 with a higher score implying creditworthiness.

Although the FICO score has been used for over 20 years as a reliable resource, it is not the deciding factor in your loan application. Each bank has its own set of criteria in granting debt to clients.

Credit Reports

❧

Every single transaction you have made as a consumer is collected in a single document called a credit report. Banks often check your report for loan applications that involve a large sum of money as a further guarantee of your creditworthiness.

The information supplied in your credit report is pooled by credit bureaus. These credit-research organizations are affiliated with financial institutions where banks pay a fee to be able to become a member. When a bank is affiliated, they give information about their customers. The credit bureau, in turn, gives access to databases that contain information about possible clients.

Take note that, the information one bank supplies will be readily available for any other bank affiliated to a credit bureau. Besides banks, other clients are mortgage lenders, insurance companies and credit card firms. There are three dominant credit bureaus trusted by banks: Equifax, Experian, and TransUnion.

What's in My Credit Report?

❧

What's in my credit report?
The information within your credit report has two categories: account data and credit reference agency files.

ACCOUNT DATA

Includes *all* information regarding every transaction you made with a bank. These comprise of:

- Monthly payment status - refers to your periodic payments. Banks are very particular about this to see whether you *pay late*.
- Account balance – banks also disclose how much debt you currently have.
- Credit Limit – Lenders also check the amount of available credit you spend. They compare your credit limit to your debts to see if you are a frequent spender.

- Account status −This is to verify the *validity* of the account. Old dormant accounts are never reliable. Lenders need to know your financial situation in the present, but they also take a brief look of your transactions in the past.

Credit reference agency files

Credit references refer to the information tied to your account. These are often filled up by consumers in their application form. Another source is the local government, which holds legal information about a client. Your credit reference also speaks about your financial security and stability.

- Address − It might look irrelevant but your address implies *stability*. Banks will become skeptical if you have multiple accounts with different addresses. They will also check whether you live in an apartment or your own house.
- Contact numbers − Your telephone line also implies stability. Banks will cross-check differences in your accounts to see if you frequently change contact numbers. Always remember that, banks think about the possibility of fleeing borrowers attempting to evade payment.
- Court records - This refer to any business made with the government. Banks will pay very close attention to your court records for it contains information about any *lawsuits* against you or if you have applied for *bankruptcy* in the past.
- Fraud − Your delinquencies such as evading payments, identity thefts and credit scams hurt

your creditworthiness, for it shows that you are irresponsible and harmful for the bank.

- Search linked data – Bankers also check if other institutions have made searches to your credit report.

It is worth mentioning that a recent new policy in the UK, allows credit bureaus access to *rental payment data*. Now, landlords also buy access to credit reports to check on possible tenants.

What's the Difference?

❧❀❧

If credit reports are already there to begin with, why are credit scores needed?

Your credit score delivers a glance of your financial status. Whenever you are applying for a loan, companies quickly check your credit score. A loan applicant having a *high credit rating* is likely to have an application approved quickly. Since you already have a good rating, banks don't need to check your reports. Conversely, applicants with lower ratings have a higher risk of rejection because banks also consult credit reports. Even if companies give you credit, they'll still go over your credit report to decide what interest rate to give you.

Having higher scores not only expedites your application, but also saves you from being looked up by banks because credit scores are also affected by how much banks are looking up your profile.

Why Your Credit Score Is Important?

T**HE IMPORTANCE OF CREDIT SCORES AND THE FALLACIES BEHIND THEM**
Your credit score means more than just your credit worthiness; it also implies your behavior and personality as a person. Having good credit also opens doors to premiums and incentives. Therefore, improving your credit is a must.

BANKS BASE YOUR INTEREST RATE ON YOUR SCORE

Assuming that you did get credit in spite of your low credit score, most likely, you will end up with a bad deal. According to myFico.com, banks calibrate the offer based on your credit score. A higher score will give you a lower interest rate while people with lower credit scores have to pay more.

myFICO's research concluded that borrowers under the 720-850 score bracket only have to pay 5.9% interest for a 30 year fixed rate loan, while clients with scores ranging from 500-559 pay as much as 9.29% interest. Having lower credit scores can definitely cost you even more!

A financial theory states that banks must impose a disincentive for borrowers to make late payments. The additional interest rate given to high-risk borrowers is called a risk premium.

INSURANCE COMPANIES HAVE THEIR OWN SCORES

Insurance is quite similar to credit because both require frequent payments. Insurance firms, likewise, have to check your credit score and credit report to quickly assess your ability to pay. Although they do consult credit bureaus, insurance companies *have their own version of a score*. Your health history and other medical related information are also included in the calculations to create a balanced assessment between financial and medical history.

Insurance rates also follow the same principle as credit interest rates, with higher scores having discounted offers.

UTILITY COMPANIES AND LANDLORDS CHECK YOUR credit score

Before granting you a phone plan or an electricity line, utility companies look up your credit score. A high credit score implies that you have debt but you are paying on time. These firms need to have assurance that the consumer has the money to pay services that are billed monthly.

Mentioned earlier was the growing trend in the UK where landlords consider your credit score. In the US, the custom is also being observed to a lesser extent. US landlords can only ask for your credit score because they have no mandate under the law.

Is Credit Important For Jobs?

Credit Scores are considered in job applications

There is a growing practice where employers run credit checks on job applicants. Especially in financial firms, every employee must be responsible with the money they handle. Credit scores can denote whether an employee is responsible with all their obligations.

A study by the Society of Human Resource Management, a business academic journal, reported that half of employers from all job sectors check credit scores of job applicants. Alongside checking your social media accounts, employers are now finding more ways to know you aside from the usual interview method.

However, Demos, another research institution, counter-argues that credit scores are not a good indicator of employee accountability. Managers should also ask the applicant the reason for a low credit score. Demos further attacks the practice by stating that applicants with low credit scores are likely to have unemployed spouses, student loans and medical debt.

It is worth mentioning that the American sub prime loan

crisis in 2010 has hampered a person's ability to get credit because of overdue accounts that have accumulated big interest. Because of the big debt, many filed for bankruptcy. Soon their homes were foreclosed and their other properties were repossessed as collateral. Their credit ratings then fell because of the amount of negative records piling up in their credit report.

Currently, there are only ten US states that ban credit checking. Nevada even gives employees the right to sue companies that turn them down due to bad credit reputation.

Even if the practice is slowly becoming obsolete, managers will always think twice before hiring people with low credit scores. If you are applying for a job in a bank, then it's best to improve you credit score because laws give consideration to financial institutions. Chicago, for example, exempts the banning of credit checks for financial companies.

The Fallacies and Myths Behind Your
Credit rating

❧❧❧

A joint survey made by the Fair Isaac Corporation (the company behind the FICO score) and Opinion Research Corporation for the Consumer Federation of America (CFA) concluded that almost half of Americans do not fully understand what a credit rating can do to their financial life.

The following are clarifications that dismiss several myths about your credit score

What Does Your Bank Know

❧❧❧

Your bank doesn't know everything
Financial institutions do not have access to the following information:

- Banks that have denied you of credit
- Criminal records
- Health history
- Parking tickets and speeding fines
- Salary
- Savings account

However, you should be aware that banks require you to fill up application forms. Even if they won't be able to get your salary and criminal information in a database, they will be able to see depending on your answers in the application form.

Furthermore, your savings account and medical history can only be accessible to lenders if they are part of a financial company that renders those services.

On the other hand, your credit score is not affected by your phone and utilities bill, since they are not credit. However, *banks have access to payment information*, thus bad history in paying utilities can harm your credit application.

Furthermore, although your energy and utility bills are *not* part of your credit score, *banks will check how well you can pay for basic necessities*. Before banks give you extra money, they make sure that you're able to live without the credit in the first place.

You have multiple credit scores

ASIDE FROM INSURANCE COMPANIES, *BANKS ALSO HAVE THEIR own way of calculating scores*. FICO scores are only used to verify the data produced. Also, you have different scores from all three major credit bureaus. Equifax calculates your score by using the Beacon system, Experian uses a system with the same name, and TransUnion uses its own Empirica method.

MOREOVER, EVERY LENDING INSTITUTION IS *SUBJECTIVE*. They all have their own standards in deciding whether you get accepted for a loan. They also decide the amount of interest rate to give you.

CREDIT SCORES ARE OBJECTIVE AND FREE FROM stereotypes

Not only is racism frowned upon as a basis for credit denial, it's illegal! Under the Equal Credit Opportunity Act (1976), discriminating debt clients on the basis of their race, ethnicity, color, social status, sex and civil status is strictly prohibited.

Personal 'inquires' are not taken against you

. . .

PREVIOUSLY, WE DISCUSSED THAT THE AMOUNT OF inquiries (searches about your credit report) affects your credit rating, but this doesn't mean that researching your own report will change your score. In fact, this practice is a *positive* way to fix your credit rating which we will further discuss in detail after this chapter.

MULTIPLE INQUIRES BY COMPANIES HAVE GRACE periods

FINANCIAL INSTITUTIONS ONLY SEND REPORTS ABOUT inquiries *once every 14 days.* If the same inquiry happens within that time frame, it will only count as *one.* With that in mind, you shouldn't be afraid to apply for multiple loans (just make sure that they are important). Be warned that the 14-day reprieve *does not apply to credit cards.*

YOUR SCORE IS INDEPENDENT FROM YOUR SPOUSE'S

YOUR CREDIT DATA IS *YOURS ALONE.* IF YOUR PARTNER HAS A debt problem, then it does not reflect on your own report as long as you two do not own a *joint debt account.* If your house is under mortgage and named under both of you, then any negative information collected from that debt will reflect on both of your reports and thus affect your credit score.

THE TRUTH ABOUT CREDIT REPAIR COMPANIES

Credit fix firms have been controversial for scamming several people with big debt. These companies promise to clear up your credit report by complaining to credit bureaus. Disputing data in credit reports is normal. But these credit repair companies abuse the power of disputing records by claiming that real factual data are wrong!

CREDIT BUREAUS QUICKLY RESPOND TO APPEALS ABOUT their data and they are smarter than you think. Challenging real data will lead to another set of watchful eyes monitoring every business transaction you make.

CREDIT REPAIR COMPANIES ARE A COMPLETE WASTE of time

Credit repair companies only attempt to change your credit record, which is unlikely to happen if there is no evidence to support the claim. Surprisingly, you can analyze your credit report and bring forward requests to the bureaus yourself! Not only will you be sure that you're sending a valid appeal, you will also personally oversee how the changes are made.

Also, quick fix schemes are going to cost you a lot. Paying $400 to run over your records is an unreasonable price when you can do it yourself. Soon enough, when you're finding them, they won't show up. It's best to avoid credit repair companies entirely.

SOME INDICATIONS THAT THEY'RE A SCAM ARE:

- They let you sign documents without giving you time to read through them

- Payment is demanded right after signing the agreement
- You sign a waiver that will give the credit repair company immunity from lawsuits
- Requires you to forge documents

In the latter part of this book, we will discuss how to fix your credit scores without having to cheat.

How did your Credit Score Get so Low?

YOU MIGHT BE WONDERING WHY YOU ARE GIVEN LOW credit grades. After understanding the components of a credit report, we are now ready to discuss how scores are computed. We'll then enumerate factors that might have led to a decline in credit score.

Calculating your credit score

Payment History 35%

Your payment history bears a lot of weight in deciding your credit score. Some of the components of payment history are mortgage, credit card debt and student loans. Credit bureaus will give higher points to borrowers that pay off loans in the agreed amount and on time. Furthermore, your recent payments whether good or bad will have more weight than past transactions.

Debt Level 30%

Formerly, your payment history was the bulk of your credit score. Now, the amount you borrow compared to your account's debt limit is almost at par with your financial history.

LENGTH OF CREDIT HISTORY 15%

As mentioned earlier, banks also consider the age of credit accounts. A good long standing relationship with another financial institution implies that the bank has done good business with you. It also gives the banks a guarantee that the client will be transacting with them for years to come. Moreover, a long history supports your financial behavior because the longer you have paid on time, the more creditworthy you are.

CREDIT INQUIRIES 10%

Whenever you apply for a new loan or credit card, an inquiry to your profile is made. Thus, a lesser number of bank account is preferred for it implies that you require minimal credit.

Moreover, when businesses look your credit report up, it also shows how many banks are checking your profile for more information. Having multiple inquiries imply that banks need further background checks before granting you credit.

MIX CREDITS 10%

YOUR ABILITY TO HAVE MANY FORMS OF CREDIT (HOUSING loan, mortgage, student loan and credit card debt) shows your *flexibility* as a borrower. It also shows that you are *experienced* in managing debt.

WHY IS MY CREDIT RATING LOW?

YOU PAID LATE

Your credit history has a track record of all your late payments. Having numerous records of late payments will reflect badly on your credit score and also your image as a responsible borrower.

What people don't know is that, banks have criteria whether or not to send a late payment report to the credit card bureau. Although it's highly encouraged to never pay late, banks will not send a late payment report if you pay within 30 days after the due date.

Even if you have a grace period and it won't show up in your record, your behavior will affect a loan application if you do a transaction with the same bank.

MAXING OUT YOUR LIMIT

Your debt relative to your limit is also a factor in your score. If you took a debt with a high value, then chances are, your score will decline.

Not meeting your maximum means that you are not a credit-holic (someone who has a tendency to make excessive debt).

It is also possible for a credit card company to lower your credit limit. This makes it easier for you to max out, and thus get lower scores.

. . .

Closing an old account

It's been proven that letting go of dormant accounts lower your FICO score especially if the account was years old. Your credit report removes any information linked to the closed account; hence, there are no data about your old financial history.

On the other hand, your score will also decline if the account was closed and it still had unpaid obligations.

Opening a new account

Conversely, opening a new account increases the number of inquiries linked to your profile. Applying for multiple credits implies that in the future you will be paying a lot of obligations, thus the bank might think that you won't be able to handle additional debt.

However, your credit score only considers new accounts opened in the current year.

The bulk of your debt are from credit cards

Revolving debt, accumulated from credit cards, significantly lowers your score. Other than that, if your obligations are only one type, banks will think that you are not experienced enough to handle debt.

Bankruptcy

Bankruptcy is a legal petition filed by either the debtor or the borrower. It is declaration of incapacity to discharge debt. Your score will decrease if you had recently filed for bankruptcy. Eventually, your bankruptcy record will be erased, but it will take ten years to do so.

· · ·

Easy Ways To Repair Your Credit Score
Fixing your credit score

Finally! By now you should have fully understood what a credit score is and why it is important. We are now going to discuss techniques to get rid of your debt and, in effect, improve your credit score.

The first part of the guide assumes that you currently have lots of debt. It will serve as a quick emergency guide towards removing you from debt and stopping your rating from decreasing.

The latter part will be a guide after you have resolved every obligation. This is the stage where you want to restore a good credit standing.

Stopping the plunge from bankruptcy and default

You have received emails, phone calls and text messages from your debtors. You now find yourself in a frustrating situation, as negative records are put into your credit report. Soon, your credit score will decline

Other than that, you are also struggling with paying off your debt. The interest has tremendously increased, leaving you with no capacity to pay.

Do not let this situation escalate further towards getting a defaulted loan and then to bankruptcy. Don't risk getting your home, property and car repossessed by banks.

The first steps involve getting your credit report and checking errors, then moving on to slowly paying up your debt by using credit payment schemes.

I. Get your credit report

CREDIT SCORES ARE REFLECTED BY THE ENTRIES IN YOUR credit report. If you are aware that you have debt from different lenders, then it's best that you get a copy of your credit report to carefully study the reasons behind your falling credit score. Under the Fair Credit Reporting Act (FCRA) borrowers are entitled one free copy of their own credit report from the three major credit bureaus.

You can get your report by using the free services of www.creditkarma.com and www.annualcreditreport.com.

1. **Check for discrepancies**

ONCE YOU HAVE YOUR REPORT, ANALYZE THEM CRITICALLY. Having a few errors in your record is normal. Be sure to check every single data and pay special notice to the date, amount of your loan and also the interest rates.

This step will take time as you might have accumulated numerous debts over the years. Be patient and leave no stone unturned.

Remember that, old debt will be cleared off if it was fully paid seven years ago. Furthermore, a wrong date can also mean a lot to your score because 35% of your score is from payment history. There are cases where old debt suddenly becomes new debt, due to a computer error. Any debt paid off years ago can still affect you, if it wasn't properly documented.

Furthermore, you can contest discrepancies in calculation, although this is unlikely, $1,000 and $10,000 are two completely different amounts of money.

List down everything and prepare all the documents linked to all faulty data. You will not win a dispute case if you don't have evidence backing you up.

I. **Dispute the erroneous data**

Once you have a list of all erroneous data, contact the credit bureau where you got your credit report. Usually, you can just email them your request, but calling them is better if you want a quick response to your concern.

Never agree that they'll update you through traditional mail. Tell them that under the terms and agreements of credit bureaus, if they do not respond to your request in 30 days, your disputed entry will be automatically deleted. This rarely happens with the three major credit bureaus but can occasionally occur to third-party companies that also collect data about your financial situation.

Once you observe that the data has been deleted, ask for a letter confirming the change. This serves as a safeguard for unpredictable events.

If you removed a number of disputed data, your credit score will significantly increase.

I. **Make a budget**

Plan everything you are going to spend-- from groceries, utilities, rent and gas. Make smart decisions as to what you really need. If possible, you should strip yourself to the complete essentials to squeeze out every possible savings you can muster.

The remainder of your money will be used in the next step.

I. **Set up a payment plan**

Right now you are buried in debt and your outstanding balance is swelling up. What you can do is use a payment plan that automatically deducts a monthly amount from your account to pay for your debt.

An alternative could be setting up two separate accounts - one for your debt payments and the other for you basic necessities.

Will you be able to pay at all?

❦

Will you be able to pay at all?

The previous options assume that you still have a stable job. If not, try negotiating with the bank. These institutions also want to get their money back and would rather talk to you first before going to a bankruptcy hearing. Strike up a payment plan; an agreement by you and the lender that you promise to pay a certain amount every month or week.

Call the creditor as soon as you know that you won't be able to make any payments. If you show sincerity, they will approve your request. You can further reinforce faithfulness by giving a copy of the budget you made.

You also can try to convince your creditors to remove the late payment charges if you will happen to miss the due date by only a few days. Just show them valid reasons for your late payments and they will take out the fees as an act of generosity.

Do not lie about your situation. Tell the lenders your status as it is. Give your apologies and promise them that you will pay back everything.

There are two methods to tackling debt: avalanching and snowballing. Avalanching is paying off the debt with the highest interest rate first before moving down to smaller balances. Snowballing is a gradual approach by starting from the bottom up. If enough funds are available to pay a large debt, then you should use the avalanche method. This will make it cheaper for you because you stop the balance from growing bigger.

OTHER METHODS OF PAYMENT

THE FOLLOWING TWO OPTIONS SHOULD ONLY BE USED IF you don't have anywhere to get your funds from.

If all else fails, borrow from yourself using your insurance. Technically you are just shifting your debt, but if you are left with no choice, this is a viable option because insurance has a lower interest rate compared to other loans. Make sure to pay back what you borrowed for it will be deducted from the money your beneficiaries will receive if you die.

Another method is applying for a credit union, which is a cooperative lending institution that offers loans at lower rates to its members. Be warned, you will not be getting enough money from the union to pay your big debts.

Keep paying on time until your debts slowly decrease. Avoid spending on your credit card and rely on real cash.

Moving Towards Improving Your Credit Scores

❦

Moving towards improving your credit scores

By now, you can suffice your needs and manage debt that's slowly getting smaller. Credit bureaus can now consider you stable but only barely. Although banks will now accept your credit score, they will only give you a deal with high interest.

Since you're just fresh from getting out of big debt, your score will be in the 400-550 range. Our next task is raising your credit score so you can get better deals. We are now rebuilding your financial standing by getting credit again slowly.

I. **Apply for a secured credit card**

MAJOR BANKS OFFER *SECURED CREDIT CARDS* THAT REQUIRE you to pay a deposit usually at $400. You can then use that deposit to pay for products. It might look like a debit card, but secured credit cards need a minimum balance to be used.

Furthermore, it will still count as debt if you don't pay your monthly due. Getting one is a great way for banks to rebuild trust in your creditworthiness.

I. **Revive your credit cards**

You may have thought about cutting off your accounts to increase your score. This is never advisable because it will end up decreasing your credit rating further by as much as 30 points. Canceling your account will not make your outstanding balances disappear. You will still have to pay for all of the debt still left.

Furthermore, keeping your old credit cards active is healthier than cancelling them. Once you cancel, all of the data linked to that account will be automatically deleted. Again, it might look promising to delete bad records, but letting another new account mature will take years.

Your debt level accounts as for 30% of your score. The higher the debt the smaller your score will be. Credit card firms are very particular with your debt-to-limit ratio. It is the amount of credit you accumulated compared to your limit. Having debt that is 30% compared to your limit shows that you are not a credit-holic and will increase your score. Having a 10% debt-to-limit ratio would further give your numbers a boost.

If you already have a stable job, you can get close to the credit limit. Then, you pay the day before the due date in full. Take note, your payments are not being monitored by accountants, but by machines. As long as you pay your dues, they will be registered. Credit bureaus will even reward you for discharging big debt by increasing your score.

If you have cancelled your credit card, then you should only apply for one. Getting 3 sets of credit cards at the same time can hurt your score because of the amount of inquiries being made to your credit report.

I. **Apply for mix credit**

Start getting new debt like car loans. Depending on your current financial stability, you may opt to apply only two new loans. Make sure to apply within a 14-day timeframe so that it will be counted as one inquiry. Getting credit aside from credit cards contributes to 10% of your credit score.

If you balance your credit usage, as well as your credit payment, the banks will record your activity. Soon you will be getting closer towards getting into the upper 700-850 credit score bracket.

JUST REMEMBER THAT GETTING OUT OF DEBT IS HARD. There is no shortcut towards removing your bad records. If you feel reluctant that you ever spent a dime on getting credit, then think again. We make mistakes, and the best way to do with them is to learn from them.

Afterword

Thank you for reading this book. I hope that you'll get to apply everything you learned here to get you out of debt and back to a good credit standing.

The process of improving your credit score roughly takes two years to complete. It takes patience to get out of this financial situation, but soon you'll enjoy premiums and incentives given by banks.